GW01045180

THE LITTLE BOOK OF

The Magic
Roundabout™

First published 2005 by Boxtree
An imprint of Pan Macmillan Ltd
Pan Macmillan, 20 New Wharf Road, London N1 9RR
Basingstoke and Oxford
Associated companies throughout the world
www.panmacmillan.com

ISBN 0 7522 2528 6

Produced under license by Magic Rights Limited

Text taken from the original TV series by Eric Thompson.

1 3 5 7 9 8 6 4 2

A CIP catalogue record for this book is available from the British Library.

Designed by seagulls

Printed by Proost, Belgium

THE LITTLE BOOK OF

The Magic
Roundabout ™

BOXTREE

'I'm here. Let joy
be unconfined.'

'I think it's going to be one of those days.'

'I'm watching these crazy mushrooms grow. Like, it's, er, it's very tiring.'

'It's going to be tears before bedtime, I know.'

'I'm terribly
confused.'

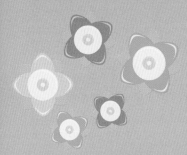

'The Flying Scot
would never have
stood for this!'

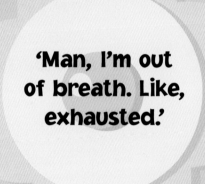

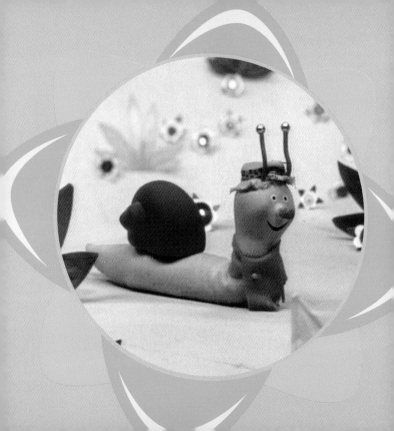

'Snails are
misused little
creatures.'

'Whatever next?'

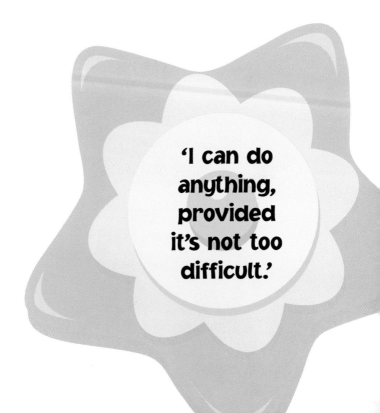

'I can do anything, provided it's not too difficult.'

'Flowers to grow,
spuds to pull
and lots of things
horticultural to
attend to.'

'After all, I'm a lady.'

'I don't know what
this garden's coming
to, I really don't.'

'You called, Madam, and I arrive. Your wish is my command.'

'I think everything will be all right, now.'

'Time for bed,
I think.'